Baby Care

From The Hospital To Your Home

Annalis de Armas RN, IBCLC

1(833) 229 0786

Latchedconsultations.com

About Me

My name is Annalis and I am a Registered Nurse and an International Board Certified Lactation Consultant. I've always had a passion to help and support others. It was during my nursing career that I discovered my truest passion and calling: helping mothers and babies. Working alongside them during those precious early days, I gained invaluable experience and knowledge about breastfeeding and all its benefits. I have helped about 19,000 mothers and look forward to helping many more. My dedication to helping mothers and families with their baby care needs and supporting them in their breastfeeding journey led me to realize there was a lack of help for mothers out there. This realization fueled my desire to create a safe and nurturing space for mothers and families, where they could confide in me and receive the help they need. I am excited to embark on this journey with you and help you achieve the best start for both you and your baby with Latched.

First Things First

- Within this book, we have provided you many of the important things you should be prepared for to care for your newborn. As you read on, you will come across LATCHED HACK'S, which are our personal tips and secrets to help you transition into becoming a new parent.
- As the arrival of your newborn gets closer, this time can be very exciting but can also be intimidating. If you are delivering your newborn in a hospital setting, here is a list of things that can help you prepare and discuss ahead of time so there are no surprises during your stay. Keep in mind, the following are optional but highly recommended by healthcare professionals.
    - Vitamin K
        - Vitamin K is an important nutrient that plays a crucial role in blood clotting. Newborn babies have low levels of vitamin K at birth, which can put them at risk for a rare but serious bleeding disorder called Vitamin K Deficiency Bleeding (VKDB). To prevent VKDB, healthcare providers typically recommend administering a vitamin K injection to newborns shortly after birth.
        - Here are some key points about vitamin K administration for newborns:
            - 1. Purpose: Vitamin K helps in the production of clotting factors in the liver, which are necessary for blood to clot properly. Newborns have lower levels of vitamin K because it does not easily pass through the placenta during pregnancy and is not produced in significant amounts by the baby's intestines. Administering vitamin K helps prevent bleeding problems in newborns.
            - 2. Timing: The vitamin K injection is usually given shortly after birth, within the first few hours or days. This timing ensures that the baby receives vitamin K protection as early as possible.

- 3. Administration: The vitamin K injection is typically given as an intramuscular injection, usually in the baby's thigh muscle. It is a quick and relatively painless procedure.
- 4. Safety: The vitamin K injection has been used for many years and is considered safe and effective in preventing VKDB.

- Erythromycin
  - Babies are sometimes given erythromycin after birth as a preventive measure against a bacterial eye infection called ophthalmia neonatorum. This infection can be caused by certain bacteria, including Chlamydia trachomatis and Neisseria gonorrhoeae, which can be present in the birth canal of an infected mother. Erythromycin is an antibiotic that is effective against these bacteria. It is typically administered as an eye ointment or eye drops shortly after birth.
  - It is a safe and widely practiced intervention to protect the newborn's eyes and prevent any potential complications that may arise from bacterial eye infections.
  - Most hospitals offer erythromycin ointment within the first 24 hours of the baby's life.
- Hepatitis B Vaccine
  - Hepatitis B is a viral infection that affects the liver. It can cause both acute and chronic liver disease and is one of the major global health problems. The virus is transmitted through contact with the blood or other body fluids of an infected person.
  - Babies need the hepatitis B vaccine because they are particularly vulnerable to the infection. If a mother is infected with hepatitis B, there is a risk of transmitting the virus to her baby during childbirth. Babies who are infected at birth have a higher risk of developing

chronic hepatitis B, which can lead to serious liver problems later in life, such as liver cirrhosis and liver cancer.

    - The hepatitis B vaccine is highly effective in preventing the transmission of the virus. By vaccinating babies at birth, they can develop immunity against the virus and significantly reduce their risk of developing hepatitis B-related complications in the future. It is a safe and essential vaccine that provides long-lasting protection against hepatitis B.
    - Most hospitals offer the first hepatitis B vaccine within the first 24 hours of the baby's life.

- Delayed Newborn Bath
    - There are potential benefits to waiting 24 hours before bathing a newborn. Here are a few reasons why some healthcare professionals recommend delaying the first bath:
        - 1. Temperature regulation: The vernix caseosa, a waxy substance that covers the baby's skin at birth, helps to regulate their body temperature. Delaying the first bath allows the vernix to remain on the skin longer, providing insulation and helping the baby maintain a stable body temperature.
        - 2. Skin protection: The vernix also acts as a natural moisturizer and protects the baby's delicate skin from drying out. It has antimicrobial properties that can help prevent infections. Waiting to bathe the newborn allows the vernix to continue moisturizing and protecting the skin.
        - 3. Early bonding: The first hours after birth are crucial for bonding between the baby and the parents. Delaying the bath allows for uninterrupted skin-to-skin contact and breastfeeding initiation, which can enhance the bonding experience and promote breastfeeding success.

- 4. Stable blood sugar levels: Some studies suggest that delaying the first bath may help stabilize the baby's blood sugar levels. Early bathing can lead to a drop in blood sugar levels, which may require additional monitoring and interventions.

- It's important to note that individual hospital practices and healthcare providers may have different recommendations regarding the timing of the first bath. It's always best to consult with your healthcare provider to determine the most appropriate approach for your baby.

- A LATCHED HACK: ASK THE HEALTHCARE PROFESSIONAL TAKING CARE OF YOUR NEWBORN IF YOU MAY WATCH THE FIRST BATH TO BE PART OF THE SPECIAL EXPERIENCE.

- Circumcision

  - The decision to circumcise a newborn is a personal one and can depend on cultural, religious, or medical factors. Most hospitals offer circumcision for a newborn during the hospital stay so it is beneficial to discuss ahead of time. Here are some potential pros and cons to consider when it comes to circumcision:

  - Pros of circumcision:

    - 1. Reduced risk of urinary tract infections (UTIs): Circumcision has been associated with a lower risk of UTIs in infants. However, the overall risk of UTIs in uncircumcised boys is still relatively low.

    - 2. Decreased risk of penile cancer: Circumcision has been linked to a reduced risk of penile cancer later in life. However, penile cancer is a rare condition, and other factors such as good hygiene and safe sexual practices also play a role in prevention.

        - 3. Easier hygiene: Some argue that circumcision makes it easier to maintain genital hygiene since the foreskin does not need to be retracted and cleaned. However, proper hygiene practices can also be taught and followed for uncircumcised individuals.
    - Cons of circumcision:
        - 1. Pain and potential complications: Circumcision is a surgical procedure that involves removing the foreskin. It can cause pain and potential complications such as bleeding, infection, or damage to the penis if not performed correctly.
        - 2. Loss of sensitivity: The foreskin contains sensitive nerve endings, and some argue that circumcision may result in a decrease in sexual sensitivity later in life. However, the impact on sexual sensation can vary among individuals.
    - It's essential to discuss the pros and cons of circumcision with your healthcare provider and consider your own beliefs, cultural background, and medical factors to make an informed decision that is best for your child.
- Newborn Birth Certificate
    - Hospitals typically provide a document called a "Birth Certificate Worksheet" or "Birth Record Worksheet" upon the birth of a newborn. This document is not the official birth certificate but contains important information about the baby and parents that will be used to register the birth and obtain the official birth certificate.
    - The Birth Certificate Worksheet is usually filled out by the parents or legal guardians at the hospital shortly after the birth. It includes details such as the baby's full name, date and time of birth, place of birth, parents' names, and other relevant information. This document serves as a record of the birth and is used as a reference when registering the birth with the appropriate government office.

- Once the Birth Certificate Worksheet is completed, it is typically submitted to the local government or vital records office responsible for birth registration. The office will then process the information provided and issue the official birth certificate.

- Some hospitals may assist with the registration process and forward the Birth Certificate Worksheet to the appropriate office on behalf of the parents, while in other cases, the parents may need to personally submit the form to the office.

- To obtain the official birth certificate, it is advisable to contact the local government or vital records office in the relevant jurisdiction for specific instructions and any additional requirements. They will be able to provide accurate information on the process, required documents, and any fees involved in obtaining the official birth certificate for the newborn.

- Newborn Health Insurance

  - In many cases, newborns are automatically covered under their parents' health insurance plans after birth. However, the specifics can vary depending on the insurance provider and policy. Here are some general points to consider:

    - 1. Parent's Insurance Policy: It is important to review the details of the parent's insurance policy to understand the coverage for newborns. Some policies may require the parents to add the newborn to the policy within a certain timeframe, such as 30 days from the date of birth, in order for the coverage to be effective.

    - 2. Enrollment Process: The parents will typically need to contact their insurance provider to enroll their newborn and provide necessary information.

    - 3. Coverage Details: Once the newborn is enrolled, they should have access to the same benefits and services as outlined in the parents' insurance policy. This can include well-baby check-ups, vaccinations, hospital stays, and other necessary medical treatments. However, it is essential to review the policy to understand any limitations, deductibles, copayments, or exclusions that may apply.

- It is recommended to contact the insurance provider directly to understand the specific requirements and procedures for adding a newborn to the parents' insurance policy. They can provide detailed information on the enrollment process, effective date of coverage, and any documentation or forms that may be required.

The Stages Of Newborn Stool

- Newborn stool goes through several stages as the baby's digestive system develops and adapts to feeding. Here are the different stages of newborn poop:
    - 1. Meconium: Meconium is the "first poop" a newborn passes. It is thick, sticky, and greenish-black in color. Meconium is composed of materials the baby ingested while in the womb, such as amniotic fluid, mucus, and skin cells. It is typically passed within 24 to 48 hours after birth. However, some may pass it before birth, especially if there was fetal distress or the baby was overdue. A LATCHED HACK: THIS FIRST POOP RESEMBLES TAR OR MOTOR OIL IN CONSISTENCY SO BE PATIENT WITH THOSE FIRST DIAPER CHANGES.
    - 2. Transitional Stool: After the meconium is passed, the baby's stool transitions to a lighter green color. This is often referred to as transitional stool. It may still have a sticky consistency but is less thick than meconium.
    - 3. Breast Milk Stool: As the baby begins to consume breast milk, the stool changes in color, consistency, and odor. Breast milk stool is usually yellow, loose, and seedy in texture. It may have a slightly sweet or sour smell. Breastfed babies tend to have stools that are more frequent and watery compared to formula-fed babies.
    - 4. Formula-fed Stool: Babies who are fed formula have slightly different stool characteristics compared to breastfed babies. Formula-fed stool is typically yellow or tan in color and has a firmer consistency than breast milk stool. It may be less frequent and have a stronger odor compared to breastfed baby stools.

Feeding Your Newborn

- Feeding a newborn baby is an important and delicate task. Here are some general guidelines on how to feed a newborn:
    - 1. Breastfeeding: If possible, breast milk is the **best source of nutrition** for a newborn. It provides all the necessary nutrients and antibodies to protect against infections. Nurse on demand, which is usually around 8-12 times a day in the first few weeks. This means you'll feed your baby every 2-3 hours, or sometimes even hourly until your milk fully comes in. A LATCHED HACK: FOLLOW UP WITH A LATCHED CONSULTANT TO ASSIST YOU WITH BREASTFEEDING.
    - 2. Bottle-feeding: If you choose to use formula, follow the instructions on the formula packaging for mixing and preparation. Use sterilized bottles and nipples. When it comes to formula feeding, feed the baby every 3-4 hours, or when they show hunger cues.
    - 3. Feeding positions: Hold your baby in a comfortable position during feeding. For breastfeeding, use the cradle hold, cross-cradle hold, or football hold. For bottle-feeding, hold your baby semi-upright with their head supported. A LATCHED HACK: FOR MORE INFORMATION, SCHEDULE A LATCHED PRENATAL VISIT.
    - 4. Keep track of feeding: It can be helpful to keep a record of your baby's feeding times, duration, and wet/dirty diapers to ensure they are getting enough nutrition. A LATCHED HACK: THIS IS VERY BENEFICIAL TO TAKE TO THE NEWBORN'S FIRST PEDIATRICIAN VISIT TO HELP THE DOCTOR ASSESS THE NEWBORN'S PROGRESS.
- Remember, every baby is unique, and their feeding needs may vary. It's important to consult with your pediatrician for personalized guidance and support.

Feeding Cues

- Look for signs that your baby is hungry, such as:
  - Smacking lips, sucking on fingers, or rooting (turning head towards the side when cheek is touched).
  - Crying is a late sign of hunger, so try to feed the baby before they get too upset.
- Look for signs that your baby is full, such as:
  - turning away from the bottle or breast, slowing down or stopping sucking, or becoming relaxed. A LATCHED HACK: RELAXED HANDS AND ARMS ARE A SIGN OF BEING FULL. A FIST CAN MEAN THEY'RE HUNGRY.

Burping

- Burping a baby is important for several reasons:
    - 1. Preventing discomfort: Babies tend to swallow air while feeding, which can lead to discomfort and gas. Burping helps release the trapped air from their stomach, reducing the chances of discomfort, bloating, and colic.
    - 2. Reducing spit-up and reflux: Burping helps to reduce the likelihood of excessive spit-up and acid reflux in babies. When air is trapped in their stomach, it can push the milk or formula back up, causing spit-up and discomfort. Burping allows the air to escape, minimizing these issues.
    - 3. Promoting better feeding: If a baby is not properly burped, they may become full quickly and stop feeding prematurely. Burping during and after feedings helps to create more space in their stomach, allowing them to continue feeding comfortably.
    - 4. Preventing ear infections: When babies swallow air while feeding, it can also cause air pressure to build up in their ears. Burping helps to release the trapped air and prevents the development of ear infections.
- To burp a baby, you can follow these steps:
    - 1. Positioning: Hold your baby in an upright position against your chest, with their chin resting on your shoulder. Alternatively, you can sit them on your lap, supporting their chest and head with one hand.
    - 2. Support their head: Make sure to support your baby's head and neck with your hand or forearm, ensuring their airway is clear and their head is stable.
    - 3. Pat or rub their back: Use your free hand to gently pat or rub your baby's back in an upward motion. Start with gentle pats and gradually increase the intensity if needed. You can also try rubbing their back in circular motions.

- 4. Change positions: If your baby doesn't burp after a few minutes, you can try changing their position. For example, you can lay them across your lap, face down, and gently pat their back.
- 5. Watch for burping signs: Look for signs that your baby is in need of burping, such as a slight release of gas or a small burp sound. You can also pay attention to their body language, such as squirming or arching their back, which may indicate the need for burping.
- 6. Repeat if necessary: If your baby doesn't burp after a few minutes, you can take a short break and then try again. Some babies may require multiple attempts to release trapped air.
- 7. During feeding, pause to burp your baby every 2-3 ounces if bottle-feeding, or when you switch breasts if breastfeeding.

Remember, every baby is different, and it may take some time to figure out the most effective burping technique for your little one. Be patient and gentle while burping to ensure your baby's comfort and safety.

A LATCHED HACK: SIT BABY ON LAP AND SUPPORT CHEST AND CHIN WITH ONE HAND AND USE OTHER HAND TO SUPPORT THE BACK. GENTLY ROCK THE BABY IN A CIRCULAR MOTION A FEW TIMES...YOU'D BE SURPRISED HOW OFTEN A BURP GETS RELEASED THIS WAY.

Diaper Change

- Changing an infant's diaper is a routine task that requires care and attention. Here's a step-by-step guide to changing an infant's diaper:
    - 1. Gather your supplies: Before you start, make sure you have all the necessary supplies within reach. These typically include a clean diaper, wipes, diaper rash cream (if needed), a changing pad or clean towel, and a change of clothes.
    - 2. Prepare the changing area: Find a safe and clean surface to change the diaper. You can use a changing table, a bed, or a padded mat on the floor. Make sure it is a comfortable and secure space.
    - 3. Wash your hands: Before you begin, thoroughly wash your hands with soap and water or use hand sanitizer to maintain hygiene.
    - 4. Lay the infant down: Carefully lay the infant on their back on the changing surface. Use one hand to hold their legs up and keep them steady. A LATCHED HACK: PLACE A CLEAN DIAPER BENEATH THE DIRTY DIAPER BEFORE EVEN BEGINNING. CHECK OUT OUR SOCIAL MEDIA FOR EXAMPLES.
    - 5. Remove the dirty diaper: Open the tabs or undo any fasteners on the dirty diaper. Gently lift the baby's legs by the ankles. A LATCHED HACK: WHEN OPENING DIRTY DIAPER, USE THE CLEANEST PART OF OF THE DIAPER, IF ANY, AND WIPE DOWN THE POOPY AND TUCK THE DIRTY DIAPER BELOW THE BABY'S BOTTOM. THEN, YOU CAN USE THAT DIRTY DIAPER AS YOUR DIRTY “STATION”.
    - 6. Clean the diaper area: Use baby wipes or a damp cloth to gently clean the diaper area, wiping from front to back. Make sure to clean the folds and creases. Pat dry with a clean cloth or let the area air dry for a few moments.
    - 7. Apply diaper rash cream (if necessary): If the baby has a diaper rash or if recommended by a pediatrician, apply a thin layer of diaper rash cream

to protect their skin. Be sure to follow the instructions on the cream and avoid applying too much.

- 8. Put on a clean diaper: Slide a clean diaper under the baby, making sure the back edge of the diaper is aligned with their waist. Bring the front of the diaper up between the baby's legs and fasten the tabs securely to the front of the diaper. Make sure the diaper is snug but not too tight. Double-check that the leg cuffs are properly positioned to prevent leaks. A LATCHED HACK: REMEMBER THAT CLEAN DIAPER THAT WAS PLACED UNDERNEATH THE DIRTY DIAPER? WELL THAT DIAPER IS THERE IN CASE THE INFANT DECIDES TO RELEASE AGAIN. TRUST US, IT WILL HAPPEN.
- 9. Dress the baby: If necessary, put on a fresh set of clothes on the baby once the clean diaper is secured.
- 10. Dispose of the dirty diaper: Roll up the dirty diaper, fasten it closed with the tabs, and dispose of it in a diaper pail or trash bin.
- 11. Wash your hands again: After changing the diaper, wash your hands thoroughly to maintain cleanliness.
- Remember, always keep a close eye on the infant during diaper changes to ensure their safety and never leave them unattended.
- A LATCHED HACK: MOST DIAPERS NOW HAVE A YELLOW LINE THAT RUNS FROM THE FRONT TO BACK OF THE DIAPER THAT TURNS BLUE ONCE THE BABY HAS PEED.

Genitalia Hygiene

- How to properly clean a female genitalia:
    - Gently clean the area: Starting from the front-to-back, gently wipe the labia (the outer lips) with the damp washcloth. Use a gentle, downward motion. Avoid wiping back and forth to prevent spreading bacteria. Be careful not to rub or irritate the delicate skin. After cleaning, pat the area dry with a clean, soft towel.

- How to properly clean a male genitalia:
    - Uncircumcised- Gently clean the genital area: Take a clean washcloth and gently wipe the genital area from front to back, being careful not to rub or irritate the skin.
        - Remember, it's important to avoid forcibly retracting the foreskin of your baby's penis. The foreskin is usually not fully retractable in infants, and forcing it can cause pain and injury. Let the foreskin naturally separate over time, which can take months or even years.
        - If you have any concerns or questions about cleaning your baby's uncircumcised genitalia, consult with your healthcare provider or pediatrician. They can provide personalized guidance based on your baby's individual needs.
    - Circumcised- Cleaning a circumcised baby's genitalia during a diaper change requires gentle care and attention. Here are the steps to properly clean the area:
        - 1. Wash your hands: Before you start, make sure your hands are clean. Wash them thoroughly with soap and warm water.
        - 2. Gather supplies: Gather all the necessary supplies before you begin. You will need warm water, mild baby soap or cleanser (optional), clean washcloths or cotton balls, and a towel.

- 3. Remove the soiled diaper: Carefully remove the soiled diaper from your baby, taking care not to spill or smear any stool or urine.
- 4. Observe the healing process: It's important to note that circumcision requires some time to heal. During the healing process, the tip of the penis may be covered with a protective dressing or ointment. Follow your doctor's instructions regarding the care and removal of the dressing or ointment.
- 5. Clean the area: Once the dressing or ointment has been removed (if applicable), gently clean the area around the penis with warm water. Use a clean washcloth or cotton ball and a mild baby soap or cleanser (if recommended by your healthcare provider). Be sure to use a gentle touch and avoid rubbing or scrubbing the area.
- 6. Rinse and pat dry: After cleaning, rinse the area with warm water to remove any soap residue. Then, pat the area dry with a clean, soft towel. Avoid rubbing the area, as this can cause irritation.
- 7. Put on a clean diaper: Once the area is dry, put on a clean diaper.

It's important to follow these steps with care and be gentle when cleaning your baby's genitalia. If you notice any signs of infection, such as redness, swelling, discharge, or if your baby seems uncomfortable, consult with your healthcare provider or pediatrician for further guidance and evaluation. They can provide personalized advice based on your baby's individual needs.

A LATCHED HACK: YOU'LL WANT TO USE A WET CLOTH TO COVER THE PENIS TO AVOID THE BABY SPRAYING YOU ON YOUR FACE...YOU WON'T REGRET THIS!

Newborn's Umbilical Cord

- When it comes to caring for a newborn's umbilical cord, it's important to keep it clean and dry until it heals completely. Here are some steps to follow:
    - 1. Avoid covering the umbilical cord: It's best to leave the umbilical cord uncovered and exposed to air as much as possible. This helps the area to stay dry and promotes healing. Avoid using tight or restrictive clothing that may rub against the belly button.
    - 2. Watch for signs of infection: Keep an eye out for any signs of infection, such as redness, swelling, discharge, or a foul odor coming from the belly button. If you notice any of these signs, consult your pediatrician for further evaluation and treatment.
    - 3. OPTIONAL- Use a belly button protector: Some parents choose to use a belly button protector, which is a small, breathable cover that is placed over the belly button to protect it from rubbing against diapers or clothing. This can be especially helpful if the baby's clothes tend to irritate the area.
    - 4. Follow your doctor's instructions: If your baby had a specific type of umbilical cord care recommended by your doctor, be sure to follow their instructions.
    - 5. Be patient: It's normal for the umbilical cord to take some time to heal completely. It typically takes around one to two weeks for the belly button stump to fall off and for the area to heal. During this time, continue to keep the area clean and dry.

Remember, every baby is different, and it's always a good idea to consult with your pediatrician if you have any concerns or questions about caring for your newborn's belly button.

Bath At Home

- Before beginning the newborn's bath, remember to be careful with the newborn's umbilical cord if it is still in place. DO NOT submerge the newborn into the bath until the umbilical cord has fallen off and the pediatrician says it is safe to do so.
- Bathing an infant baby can be a special and bonding experience. Here are the steps to properly bathe an infant baby:
    - 1. Gather supplies: Before you begin, gather all the necessary supplies. You will need a baby bathtub or basin, warm water (around 37°C or 98.6°F), mild baby soap or cleanser, soft washcloths, a towel, clean clothes, a clean diaper, and any other bath accessories you may want to use, such as a baby brush or sponge.
    - 2. Prepare the bathing area: Choose a safe and comfortable location for bathing your baby. This can be a baby bathtub placed on a stable surface or a basin lined with a towel to provide a soft surface. Ensure the area is warm and free from drafts.
    - 3. Fill the bathtub with warm water: Fill the baby bathtub or basin with warm water, making sure it's not too hot. Test the water temperature with an elbow or a bath thermometer to ensure it feels comfortably warm. The water level should be shallow, covering your baby's body but not submerging them.
    - 4. Undress your baby: Undress your baby completely.
    - 5. Support your baby's head and neck: With one hand supporting your baby's head and neck, gently lower them into the bathtub or basin. Keep a firm grip on your baby at all times to prevent any accidents.
    - 6. Wash your baby's body: Wet a soft washcloth with warm water and use it to gently wash your baby's body, starting from their face and working your way down. Use a mild baby soap or cleanser sparingly, avoiding the eyes and mouth. Pay special attention to the folds of the skin, neck, armpits, and diaper area.

  - 7. Shampoo your baby's hair: If your baby has hair, use a small amount of mild baby shampoo to gently cleanse their scalp. Support their head with one hand and pour warm water over their head to rinse off the shampoo. You want to avoid water entering their eyes or ears.
  - 8. Rinse your baby: Use a clean washcloth or your hand to rinse off the soap from your baby's body and hair. Make sure to remove all the soap residue, as it can cause irritation.
  - 9. Lift your baby out of the water: With one hand supporting your baby's head and neck, lift them out of the bathtub or basin and wrap them in a towel. Keep their head higher than their body to prevent water from entering their ears.
  - 10. Dry and dress your baby: Gently pat your baby dry with a soft towel, paying extra attention to the folds of their skin. Avoid rubbing, as it can cause irritation. Once dry, dress your baby in clean clothes and put on a fresh diaper.
- Remember, never leave your baby unattended during bath time, even for a second. It's important to be present and focused on your baby's safety throughout the entire bathing process. Enjoy this special time with your little one and make it a soothing and enjoyable experience for both of you.

Clothing Change

- Changing an infant's clothes may seem like a simple task, but it requires some care and attention. Here's a step-by-step guide on how to properly change an infant's clothes:
    - 1. Choose the right clothes: Select an outfit appropriate for the weather and the baby's comfort. Make sure the clothes are clean, soft, and easy to put on and take off.
    - 2. Find a safe and comfortable space: Look for a clean and flat surface to change the baby's clothes. A changing table, bed, or padded mat on the floor can be suitable options. Ensure that the area is secure and free from any hazards.
    - 3. Prepare the necessary items: Gather all the items you'll need, including a clean set of clothes, a clean diaper (if needed), wipes, and any other accessories like socks or hats.
    - 4. Lay the baby down: Gently lay the baby on their back on the changing surface. Use one hand to support their head and neck while keeping them secure.
    - 5. Remove the current clothes: Carefully undress the baby, starting with the top layer of clothing. If there are snaps, buttons, or zippers, undo them gently to avoid discomfort. Lift the baby's arms and legs as needed to remove the clothes.
    - 6. Clean and change the diaper (if needed): If the baby's diaper needs changing, follow the steps mentioned (page 16-17) to remove the dirty diaper, clean the diaper area, and put on a fresh diaper.
    - 7. Put on the new clothes: Take the clean set of clothes and gently slide them onto the baby's body. Start with the arms and then the legs, being careful not to force the baby's limbs into the clothing. If necessary, stretch the neck of the garment to fit it over the baby's head.

  - 8. Secure the closures: Fasten any buttons, snaps, or zippers on the clothes to ensure a proper fit. Be mindful of not pinching the baby's skin while closing the clothing.
  - 9. Double-check for comfort and safety: Ensure that the clothes are not too tight or loose, and that the baby is comfortable. Check that there are no tags or rough seams that might irritate the baby's skin.

- Remember, changing an infant's clothes should be done with care and attention to keep the baby comfortable and safe. Always supervise the baby during the process to prevent any accidents.

Swaddling

- Swaddling an infant can help them feel secure and calm. Here's a step-by-step guide on how to swaddle an infant:
    - 1. Start with a large, thin blanket or a specifically designed swaddle blanket.
    - 2. Lay the blanket on a flat surface, forming a diamond shape, with one corner pointing towards you.
    - 3. Fold the top corner of the blanket down about six inches to create a straight edge.
    - 4. Place your baby on the blanket with their head above the folded edge.
    - 5. Take the left corner of the blanket and gently wrap it across your baby's chest, tucking it under their right arm. A LATCHED HACK: TUCK THE BABY'S LEFT HAND INTO THE POCKET OF THE LEFT CORNER.
    - 6. Bring the bottom corner of the blanket up and over your baby's feet, tucking it behind their shoulder.
    - 7. Lastly, take the right corner of the blanket and wrap it across your baby's chest, securing it under their left arm. A LATCHED HACK: GENTLY TUCK THE BABY'S RIGHT HAND INTO THE POCKET OF THE RIGHT CORNER.
- Remember to make sure the swaddle is snug but not too tight, allowing your baby's hips and legs to move freely. Swaddling should only be done during sleep or rest time, and you should always monitor your baby to ensure they aren't overheating.
- Ensure the baby's face never gets covered by the swaddle blanket.

Newborn Soothing

- Soothing a newborn can be a comforting and bonding experience for both you and your baby but can also be a challenging experience at times. Here are some techniques to help soothe your newborn:
    - 1. Swaddling: Wrap your baby snugly in a soft blanket, mimicking the feeling of being in the womb. This can help your baby feel secure and calm.
    - 2. Gentle rocking or bouncing: Hold your baby close and gently rock or bounce them in your arms. The rhythmic motion can be soothing and help your baby relax.
    - 3. Skin-to-skin contact: Hold your baby against your bare chest, allowing them to feel your warmth and heartbeat. This can provide a sense of security and promote bonding. A LATCHED HACK: OTHER PARENT OR CLOSE FAMILY MEMBER CAN ALSO PROVIDE SKIN-TO-SKIN TO HELP SOOTH THE BABY AND BOND.
    - 4. Shushing sounds: Make a gentle "shushing" sound. This mimics the sounds they heard in the womb and can be comforting.
    - 5. Sucking: Offer your baby a pacifier or allow them to nurse if they are hungry. Sucking can have a calming effect on babies.
    - 6. White noise: Use a white noise machine or play soft, calming sounds like ocean waves or gentle lullabies. This can help drown out other noises and create a soothing environment.
    - 7. Gentle massage: Gently massage your baby's back, arms, and legs using soft, slow strokes. This can help relax their muscles and promote a sense of calm.
    - 8. Dim the lights: Create a calm and soothing environment by dimming the lights in the room. This can help your baby feel more relaxed and ready for sleep.

- 9. Take a walk or car ride: The gentle motion of a stroller or car can often have a soothing effect on babies. Taking a walk or going for a short drive can help calm your baby.

- Remember, every baby is unique, so it may take some time to find the techniques that work best for your little one. Trust your instincts and respond to your baby's cues and needs. If you're ever concerned about your baby's well-being or if they're inconsolable, it's always a good idea to consult with your pediatrician for guidance.

Infant Safety

- Here are some important tips for infant safety:
    - 1. Safe sleep practices: Always place your baby on their back to sleep, on a firm and flat surface, such as a crib or bassinet. Avoid using pillows, blankets, or stuffed animals in the sleep area, as they can pose suffocation risks.
    - 2. Crib safety: Make sure the crib meets safety standards, with slats that are no more than 2 3/8 inches apart. Use a firm mattress that fits snugly in the crib and avoid using crib bumpers, as they can increase the risk of suffocation.
    - 3. Car seat safety: Use a rear-facing car seat in the back seat of the car, and make sure it is installed correctly according to the manufacturer's instructions. Keep your baby in a rear-facing car seat until they reach the height and weight limits recommended by the seat's manufacturer.
    - 4. Prevent falls: Always supervise your baby during tummy time, and never leave them unattended on elevated surfaces such as changing tables or sofas. Use safety gates at the top and bottom of stairs to prevent falls.
    - 5. Babyproofing: Babyproof your home by covering electrical outlets, securing furniture to the wall to prevent tipping, and keeping small objects and choking hazards out of reach.
    - 6. Bathing safety: Never leave your baby unattended during bath time, even for a moment. Use a bath seat or support to keep your baby secure, and test the water temperature before placing your baby in the bath to avoid scalding. A LATCHED HACK: TO CHECK THE TEMPERATURE OF THE WATER, DIP YOUR ELBOW INTO THE WATER. THE ELBOW IS MORE SENSITIVE TO HEAT THAN A HAND.
    - 7. Prevent burns: Keep hot liquids, such as coffee or tea, away from your baby's reach. Check the temperature of formula or breast milk before feeding to avoid burns.

- 8. Sun protection: Protect your baby from the sun's harmful rays by keeping them in the shade, dressing them in lightweight, loose-fitting clothing that covers their skin, and applying sunscreen to exposed areas (if recommended by your pediatrician).
- 9. Temperature regulation: Babies are more sensitive to extreme temperatures. Keep the room temperature comfortable and dress your baby appropriately for the weather. Avoid overheating or overcooling your baby, and never leave them in a hot car, even for a short period of time. A LATCHED HACK: IT IS RECOMMENDED TO SET THE AC OF YOUR HOUSE TO 72 DEGREES FOR THE FIRST MONTH OF NEWBORN'S LIFE.
- 10. Pet safety: If you have pets at home, supervise their interactions with your baby. Teach your pets to be gentle and avoid leaving them alone with your baby. It's essential to create a safe and harmonious environment for both your baby and your pets. A LATCHED HACK: WHEN BABY IS BORN, TAKE HOME WITHIN THE FIRST 24 HOURS A SHIRT OR BLANKET THAT THE BABY WORE AND HAVE YOUR PET SMELL THE SCENT BEFORE YOU BRING THE BABY HOME TO MEET YOUR PET.
- 11. Choking hazards: Keep small objects, coins, and other choking hazards out of your baby's reach. Cut food into small pieces and closely supervise your baby during mealtime.
- 12. Poison prevention: Keep household cleaning supplies, medications, and other chemicals out of reach and locked away. Install carbon monoxide and smoke detectors in your home. **POISON CONTROL PHONE NUMBER: 1(800)-222-1222**
- 13. Regular check-ups: Schedule regular well-baby check-ups with your pediatrician to monitor your baby's growth and development and address any safety concerns.
- 14. Mental health support: Remember to prioritize your own mental health as well. Seek support from your partner, family, or friends, and reach out for professional help if needed. Taking care of yourself is crucial for providing a safe and nurturing environment for your baby.

  - A LATCHED HACK: BE AWARE OF THE NEAREST HOSPITAL BEFORE THE BABY IS EVEN BORN.

- Remember, these tips are meant to provide general guidance, and it's important to consult with your pediatrician or healthcare provider for personalized advice and recommendations based on your baby's specific needs.

Sudden Infant Death Syndrome (SIDS)

- It is the sudden and unexplained death of a seemingly healthy infant, typically during sleep. SIDS is a tragic and devastating event that can occur in babies under the age of one, usually between one and four months old.
- The exact cause of SIDS is still unknown, but there are certain risk factors associated with it. These risk factors include:
  - 1. Sleeping position: Placing a baby on their stomach or side increases the risk of SIDS. It is recommended to always put babies to sleep on their back.
  - 2. Soft bedding: Having soft bedding, such as pillows, blankets, or stuffed animals, in the crib can increase the risk of suffocation. It is advised to keep the crib free from any loose items.
  - 3. Co-sleeping: Sharing a bed with a baby increases the risk of SIDS. It is recommended to have the baby sleep in a separate crib or bassinet in the same room as the parent.
  - 4. Smoking exposure: Exposure to cigarette smoke, both during pregnancy and after birth, increases the risk of SIDS. It is important to maintain a smoke-free environment for the baby.
  - 5. Overheating: Overheating can be a risk factor for SIDS. It is important to dress the baby in appropriate clothing for the room temperature and avoid excessive layers of clothing or heavy blankets.
  - 6. Breastfeed if possible: Breastfeeding has been shown to reduce the risk of SIDS. If possible, exclusive breastfeeding is recommended for the first six months of life.
  - 7. Offer a pacifier at sleep time: Giving a pacifier at naptime and bedtime has been associated with a reduced risk of SIDS. If you are breastfeeding, wait until breastfeeding is well-established before introducing a pacifier.

- Following these guidelines can help reduce the risk of SIDS, although it's important to note that SIDS cannot be completely prevented. It is always recommended to discuss any concerns or questions about SIDS with a healthcare professional.

Newborn Emergencies

- There are several newborn emergencies that require immediate medical attention. Here are a few examples:
    - 1. Difficulty breathing: If a newborn is struggling to breathe or experiencing rapid, shallow breathing, it is considered a medical emergency.
    - 2. Cyanosis: Cyanosis is a bluish discoloration of the skin, lips, or nails. If a newborn exhibits cyanosis, it may indicate a lack of oxygen and requires immediate medical attention.
    - 3. Seizures: Seizures in newborns can be a sign of a serious underlying condition and should be treated as an emergency.
    - 4. High fever: A fever above 100.4°F (38°C) in a newborn (0-3 months) should be considered a medical emergency.
    - 5. Excessive vomiting or diarrhea: If a newborn is consistently vomiting or having frequent episodes of watery diarrhea, it could lead to dehydration and requires urgent medical attention.
    - 6. Unresponsiveness or lethargy: If a newborn is unusually sleepy, unresponsive, or difficult to wake up, it could be a sign of a serious medical condition and should be addressed immediately.
- It is important to remember that this is not an exhaustive list, and any significant change in a newborn's behavior, appearance, or health should be evaluated by a healthcare professional without delay.

Newborn Fever

- If your newborn has a fever, it's important to take it seriously and seek medical attention promptly. Here are some steps to follow when a newborn has a fever:
    - 1. Check the temperature: Use a reliable thermometer to measure your baby's temperature. Rectal thermometers are most accurate for newborns. A fever is generally defined as a rectal temperature of **100.4°F (38°C) or higher in newborns. If an infant is 0-3 months with this temperature, call the doctor and go to the ER.**
    - 2. Contact your pediatrician: Call your baby's pediatrician immediately to report the fever and seek guidance. They will provide specific instructions based on your baby's age, medical history, and other symptoms.
    - 3. Dress your baby appropriately: Avoid overdressing your baby if they have a fever. Dress them in lightweight, breathable clothing to help regulate their body temperature.
    - 4. Offer fluids: If your baby is breastfeeding or bottle-feeding, continue to offer them fluids. It's important to keep them hydrated, especially if they're experiencing a fever.
    - 5. Keep your baby comfortable: Create a calm and soothing environment for your baby. Keep the room temperature comfortable and use a soft cloth or lukewarm sponge to gently cool their body if recommended by the pediatrician.
    - 6. Follow medical advice: Once you have spoken with your baby's pediatrician, carefully follow their instructions. They may recommend bringing your baby in for an examination or suggest over-the-counter fever-reducing medication if appropriate for the baby's age.
- Remember, it's crucial to consult with a healthcare professional when your newborn has a fever. They will provide the best guidance and ensure the health and well-being of your baby.

CPR Recommendations

- What is CPR?
  - Infant CPR, or Cardiopulmonary Resuscitation, is a life-saving technique used to revive a newborn baby who is not breathing or experiencing a cardiac arrest. It involves a series of steps that aim to restore the flow of oxygenated blood to the baby's vital organs. Newborn CPR typically includes techniques such as chest compressions, rescue breaths, and clearing the airway obstruction if necessary.
  - FACT: after approximately 4-6 minutes without oxygen, brain cells can start to suffer irreversible damage. *START CPR AS SOON AS POSSIBLE**
- Causes for a child's heartbeat and breathing to stop:
  - Choking, drowning, asthma attacks, cardiac issues, head traumas/accidents, sudden infant death syndrome (SIDS), drug overdose or poisoning

CPR FOR INFANTS

LATCHED GUIDE

IF YOU ARE ALONE WITH THE INFANT GIVE 2 MINUTES OF CPR BEFORE CALLING 911.

1 SHOUT AND TAP

Shout and gently tap the child on the shoulder.
If there is no response and not breathing or not breathing normally, position the infant on his or her back and begin CPR.

2 GIVE 30 COMPRESSIONS

Give 30 gentle chest compressions at the rate of at least 100 per minute. Use two or three fingers in the center of the chest just below the nipples.
Press down approximately one-third the depth of the chest (about 1 and a half inches).

3 OPEN THE AIRWAY

Open the airway using a head tilt lifting of chin.
Do not tilt the head too far back

4 GIVE 2 GENTLE BREATHS

If the baby is not breathing or not breathing normally, cover the baby's mouth and nose with your mouth and give 2 gentle breaths. Each breath should be 1 second long. You should see the baby's chest rise with each breath.

5 REPEAT

Continue the cycles of 30 chest compressions followed by 2 rescue breaths until help arrives or baby begins to breathe on their own.

How To Save A Child From Choking

- Choking incidents in newborns can occur when small objects or food block their airway. It is important for parents and caregivers to be vigilant and create a safe environment for the newborn to prevent choking hazards. Learning proper techniques for handling a choking emergency can make a significant difference in saving the newborn's life.

HOW TO SAVE A CHILD FROM CHOKING

LATCHED GUIDE

DETERMINE IF THE INFANT IS TRULY CHOKING BY LOOKING FOR SIGNS SUCH AS DIFFICULTY BREATHING, INABILITY TO CRY OR COUGH, AND A CHANGE IN SKIN COLOR (TURNING RED OR BLUE).

1. LOOK INSIDE MOUTH

Never put your finger in a choking baby's mouth until you visually check for an obstructing object.

Pull the baby's jaw open to look inside his mouth. If you can see an object, avoid pushing it further back in the throat by sweeping a finger along the inside cheek and back behind the obiect to pop it out.

2. FIVE BACK BLOWS

If the obiect is too far back in the throat to see or easily remove with a finger, support your baby's head with his head lower than his bottom.
Using the heel of your hand, give 5 blows between the shoulder blades. Visually check for an object in the baby's mouth and remove if possible..

3. CHEST THRUSTS

If his airway is still blocked after 5 back blows, turn your baby onto his back on a firm surface and give him up to 5 chest thrusts.
Place two fingers on the breastbone just below the nipple line.
Push downward and upward (towards baby's head).
After each thrust, visually check for an object in baby's mouth and remove if possible.

4. REPEAT CYCLE

If airway is still blocked after 5 chest thrusts, repeat 3 cycles of back blows and chest thrusts before calling 911 for an ambulance. Continue the cycles until airway clears or help arrives.

Conclusion

Congratulations, you have reached the end of Latched Baby Care From The Hospital To Your Home. By now, hopefully you feel more prepared for your baby to arrive! Feel free to use this book to refer back to when you feel any doubts. Remember to trust your gut and to believe in yourself; you'll be great! Your baby loves you already and you will be perfect in their eyes no matter what. There's no handbook for becoming a first time parent but this is as good as it gets. With all your Latched Hacks, you got this! For more information, visit our website latchedconsultation.com